MW00914392

"All those who love prose and poetry will love the rhyme and rhythm of this collection by Diana Hughes. Through much pain and adversity she has given life through her words. I think this work could be used as a great daily devotional to start off each day or something to read just before you lay down to sleep. Whether you use it to begin your day or to end it, the words will truly be inspiring to you."

-Bishop Michael S. Pitts
Senior Pastor
Cornerstone Church

"Good Morning Beautiful is a wonderful collection of poems about love, faith, relationships and enduring. The poems were written with a great deal of passion and they will elevate the spirit of all who read them."

-Jerry Jones
President
Woodlands Consulting

GOOD MORNING
Beautiful

To John & Hay
Two beautiful ones!
Thanks for your prayers!
D Hughes

DIANA L. HUGHES

Wasteland Press
Shelbyville, KY USA
www.wastelandpress.net

Good Morning Beautiful
by Diana L. Hughes

Copyright © 2009 Diana L. Hughes
ALL RIGHTS RESERVED

First Printing—November 2009
ISBN: 978-1-60047-375-3
Back cover photo by Joseph Vogt – jsvogt@me.com

NO PART OF THIS BOOK MAY BE REPRODUCED IN ANY
FORM, BY PHOTOCOPYING OR BY ANY ELECTRONIC OR
MECHANICAL MEANS, INCLUDING INFORMATION
STORAGE OR RETRIEVAL SYSTEMS, WITHOUT
PERMISSION IN WRITING FROM THE COPYRIGHT
OWNER/AUTHOR

Printed in the U.S.A.

DEDICATION

This book is dedicated to my amazing Mom, Mary L. Love-Pittman, and to the love of my life, my Husband, Lawrence J. Hughes. This book is a tribute to their memories. My Mom, Mary L. Love-Pittman succumbed to cancer in February, 2002. She was the loving thread in the fabric of our family that held everything together.

My husband, Lawrence J. Hughes, gave his support and encouragement to me over the years in compiling this set of poems. I had my own personal sounding board right there in the comfort of our living room. He listened as I read and helped me to critique these poems. It never dawned on me that Lawrence would not be here to share this joy. He passed in August, 2007, also from cancer.

My Mom and Lawrence are not here to see the completion and publication of this book. Lawrence used to smile and give a thumbs up after I read a poem to him. Now I believe Lawrence and Mom both are among the cloud of witnesses peering down from the corridors of heaven; smiling, nodding with approval, and cheering me on!

They were two of the most influential people in my life who I love and miss tremendously. Both told me to, "Never Give Up On Your Dream."

ACKNOWLEDGEMENTS

I give thanks to
My Lord and Savior, Jesus Christ,
The author and finisher of my faith.
Without You I would not have:
a purpose to fulfill;
a destiny to reach;
or a dream to come true.

To Children: Tela Jordan, DeLisa Jordan, Steve Jordan, Stacey Jordan-Cooks, Ebony Hughes-Gordon. To: my grandchildren who encouraged me to finish this book.

To: The Hughes and Love Families.

Countless friends and loved ones too numerable to name. You know who you are. I will always remember your words of wisdom and prayers.

Special thanks to: Rosie Hollins, Janet Devriendt, Dr. Lisa Chavers, and Pamala Matthews for their contributions to this book.

TABLE OF CONTENTS

Part Three: Encouraging

PREFACE

Good Morning Beautiful

Our Mom was diagnosed with breast cancer in 1999 and began to receive chemotherapy treatments soon thereafter. One of the side effects she experienced was the loss of her hair. She was a beautiful proud black woman with shoulder length black tresses mingled with traces of silver. She looked much younger than 77 years of age. People actually believed our *mom* was our *sister*! She loved looking good so when she began losing her hair from the radiation sessions, she began to wear colorful scarves to cover her head.

I arrived at her house early one morning to run an errand for her. When she answered the door she was not wearing a scarf. I saw that her once beautiful, curly hair had disappeared. A scalp almost completely bare had replaced it. I thought I had prepared myself for that moment. I was wrong. I was totally caught off guard and confronted with an overwhelming sadness and reality that almost took my breath away. A mixture of emotions rushed through my heart in that split second which seemed to linger forever. I don't know if she read my mind at that moment, but before I could think of what to say, I smiled and heard these three words flowing tenderly from my lips, "Good morning Beautiful!"

At first she seemed surprised then somewhat annoyed. "Not me, I'm not beautiful." I told her, "Mom, yes you are. You are now and always will be." We both embraced each other and began to softly cry. I don't remember how long we stood there…one trying to console the other.

What took place in the next few minutes I still don't understand to this day. We started laughing! We laughed so hard that we had to dry our eyes all over again. The fears and uncertainties of the future became insignificant to us and we felt an incredible peace. This time belonged to us!

From that moment on, there was not a day that went by I didn't call her to say, "Good morning, Beautiful."

INTRODUCTION

God's Way is the Only Way

Have you ever made a *wrong* turn onto a one way street, or *missed* a turn and had to go out of your way to get back? Sometimes we all make U turns on the path of life. We yield the right of way to naysayers or people who do not understand our passion and purpose. Don't allow *just anyone* to speak into your life. God has already given us the road map and instructions regarding how to get to where we need to be. That road map is the Holy Bible…God's Divine Word.

Procrastination and placing limitations on ourselves will cause us to follow the detour signs instead of pursuing our goals. This happened to me. I knew this book was God-inspired. These poems and writings have been tested and proven true for myself and many others as our paths have crossed. However, it took me five years to complete this work. Five years of putting it off for one reason or another.

I pray that as you stand at that intersection of your life uncertain of which way to go, as I was; these writings will inspire, challenge, and encourage you. God wants us to choose the right direction and to walk in His plan.

"Trust in the Lord with all thine heart; and lean not unto thine own understanding. In all thy ways acknowledge Him, and He shall direct thy paths." (Proverbs 3:5,6-KJV)

PART ONE

Inspiring

Through God's Eyes

Look at me through God's eyes.
For your eyes can only see.
The outer shell of who I am.
A mere glimpse of who I shall be.

God is smoothing out rough edges.
Making me fit for His purpose.
There is still more work to be done.
You are looking at a work in progress.

Sometimes I have failed
When I tried to do my best.
Sometimes I did not make the grade
And did not pass the test.

Some things I have lost.
Some things I have gained.
But I paid at great cost.
Only God knows my sunshine and rain.

So don't look at my present state
Or what I'm going through.
Look at me through God's eyes.
And I'll do the same when I look at you.

"Man looks at the outward appearance,
but the Lord looks at the heart."
(I Samuel 16:7-NIV)

Lord You Are

The answer to every question.
The hope to every dream.
The object of my affection.
The wind beneath my wings.

The peace in time of sorrow.
The joy that floods my soul.
The thread that mends a broken heart.
The love that makes it whole.

"But thou, O Lord, art a shield for me;
my glory, and the lifter of mine head."
(Psalm 3:3- KJV)

Pale In Comparison

The stars in the sky
Shine as twinkling lights
For every eye to see.

The mountains so high
In their majesty rise
To the heavens gloriously.

Creation shows forth
Its awesome display
Its beauty takes our breath away.

Lord we marvel at their splendor.
Give them their reverence due.
But of everything…that our eyes have seen.
They pale in comparison to You.

"Yours, O Lord, is the greatness and the power
and the glory and the majesty and the splendor,
for everything in heaven and earth is yours."
(1 Chronicles 29:11-NIV)

Daybreak

Just before the break of day
When all is quiet and still.
And nature's morning symphony
Is the only song I hear.

Just before the many sounds
Of daily life are heard.
Before the phone starts ringing.
Before the spoken words.

I start the day with prayer
And meditation with my Lord.
A precious time of communion
With just Him and me alone.

"Give us each day our daily bread."
(Luke 11:3-NIV)

Be Still

I will cast the cares
Of this world upon You.
Silence the thoughts
That my mind pursues.

Make quiet the issues that
Entangle my heart.
I will be still…
And know that You are God.

For I can't hear You
Above the noise
Of worthless chatter
That leaves me void.

I won't allow anything
To hinder Your voice.
I will be still…
And know that You are God.

Be still and know that
He is God.
O restless soul
That pursues His heart.

And don't grow weary
While you wait.
He will show Himself mighty
As you seek His face.

"Be still before the Lord and wait patiently
for Him." (Psalm 37:7-NIV)

The Secret Place

I know just where to find You.
I know just where You are.
I know that You're not hiding.
I don't have to search from afar.

For there is a secret place.
Where Your glory is revealed.
I dwell there unafraid.
As I seek Your perfect will.

A habitation you provide.
A shield of safety at my side.
A refuge from the storm.
Your covering keeps me warm.

A place of contentment.
A place of perfect peace.
A place of no limits.
The secret place with Thee.

*"...pray to thy Father which seeth
in secret..." (Mat. 6:6-KJV)*

I Can't Stop Thinking Of You

Every second, every moment
All the time that's in between.
From early morning sunrise
To twilight's beckoning.

Thoughts overwhelm me
They remind me of Your love.
Peace beyond understanding
Grants me favor from above.

My eyes are closed to rest
I lay here quiet and still.
My heart is dancing yet
My spirit is overfilled.

When I arise tender mercies await.
Your compassion never ends.
 I get to start a brand new day
To think about You all over again.

"But his delight is in the law of the Lord
and on His law he meditates day and night..."
(Psalm 1:2-NIV)

Who Do I Turn To?

Who do I turn to
Unless it is to You?
The greatest source I know
Of undisputed truth.

You guide me with
Your light of wisdom overflowing,
And set my footing sure
On the path I should be going.

"I will bless the Lord who counsels me;
He gives me wisdom in the night.
He tells me what to do."
(Psalm 16:7-Living Bible)

There Are No Words

There are no words
To say how I feel.
There are no words
To express my love for You.

No words have been created.
Neither do they exist.
To describe Your infinite power.
Or Your great faithfulness.

Nothing that I've heard or seen.
Ever imagined, ever dreamed.
Totally reveals Your majesty.
Everything You mean to me.

I could say You are wonderful.
I could say its You I adore.
But Lord to me…You're that
And so much more…
There are just no words.

*"…and to experience this love for yourselves,
though it is so great that you will never see
the end of it or fully know or understand it.
(Ephesians 3:19-Living Bible)*

Enough to Know It's You

Lord You manifest Your love
In many different ways.
You have a way to reveal
Just what needs to be heard.

Sometimes it's through a word
Or in the melody of a song.
Sometimes a child's small voice.
Or in the midst of a quiet storm.

In a gentle breeze that rushes by
Or a beautiful sunset in the sky.
You know just how to reach us
And impart to us Your truth.

To get our utmost attention.
Enough for us to know that it is You.

"He who forms the mountains, creates the wind,
and reveals his thoughts to man…"
(Amos 4:13-NIV)

I Don't Want To Leave This Place

There is a presence here.
That my eyes cannot see.
A stirring in the air.
It fills me with expectancy.

The atmosphere is charged.
I am ready to receive.
Lord I can hardly wait
For what You have in store for me.

I don't want to leave this place.
I just want to seek Your face.
I don't want to move.
I don't want to lose.
What I have received from You.

This is where I want to stay.
Lord here at Your feet I lay.
It's where I want to be.
Where the river's flowing free.
I don't want to leave.

*"You will fill me with joy in Your
presence, with eternal pleasures at
Your right hand."(Psalm 16:11-NIV)*

The Best Part of Waking Up

The best part of waking up
Is knowing God is there.
He awaits with tender mercies
To guide me through my day.

 His veil of loving-kindness
Cloaks around me like a cover.
A fortress that sustains me
In every trial that I encounter.

His compassion fails me not.
His faithfulness is sure.
He upholds His promises by His word.
In His watch I am secure.

*"Great is His faithfulness; His loving- kindness
begins afresh each day."*
(Lamentations 3:23-Living Bible)

The Joy That Fills My Soul

You are the one that I adore.
You are the one that I live for.
In You I live, move, have my being.
Because of You…I walk in true freedom.

You are the song that stirs my heart.
You are the light shining through my dark.
You are the one that gives life its meaning.
Because of You I now soar like an eagle.

Conquering every mountain high.
Triumphing over every obstacle.
Living for You is my heart's desire.
You are the joy that fills my soul.

"You have made known to me the path of life;
You will fill me with joy in your presence…"
(Psalm 16:11-NIV)

I Am So Glad

God knew me before
I came into being.
The road I would take.
The steps I would make.
Yet He chose to love me.

He looked far ahead
To prepare my way.
So if by chance I went astray.
The path where love and mercy abounds
Could so easily by me be found.

Then as if that weren't enough.
For He knew my journey would be rough.
He gave His only begotten Son.
So I would never have to run
From the enemy and all his wiles.

I am so glad, my Father,
To be called Your child.

"For I know the plans I have for you, declares the Lord,
plans to prosper you and not harm you, plans to give
you hope and a future."
(Jeremiah 29:11-NIV)

The Magnificent Exchange

Jesus never said a word
Yet in His silence set us free.
He chose not to save Himself.
He chose to save you and me.

He could summon a host of angels
To intervene at His command.
He knew His destiny as Savior…
His fate was not in His hands.

For God's divine plan to succeed.
Jesus bore our reproach and shame.
Oh what a priceless contribution!
What a magnificent exchange!

He gave His life for you and me.
Can you imagine such a thing?
Bearing the weight of our iniquities
On His shoulders as He hang?

Wearing a crown of thorns
The soldiers had woven into a ring.
They mocked and ridiculed Him,
"Save Yourself, if You are a King!!"

They crucified our Lord that day.
They nailed Him to a cross.
Our guilt and shame all died that day.
His precious blood covered them all.

Then behold! There came a darkness
That spread across the earth's face.
The veil of the temple was suddenly
Split…from its crest to its base!

Surely this was the Son of God
They all began to say.
And the scriptures were fulfilled
When Jesus arose on the third day!

Jesus never said a word
Yet in His silence set us free.
Now we are counted as righteous
And have life eternally!

"For God so loved the world, that He gave
His one and only begotten Son,
that whosoever believeth in Him should not perish,
but have everlasting life."
(John 3:16-KJV)

Roses in a Basket

As we walked into the
church that day
And just inside the door.
Stood two ladies handing
out flowers.
Asking each of us…what color?

They were roses in a basket
for a Mother's Day delight.
The white ones stood for death.
The red ones stood for life.

I chose a red rose just for me
and held it in my hand.
Then I picked two more roses.
One for Mom, another for Gram.

I pinned them on their dresses.
Mom and Gram both smiled at me.
I said, "We'll always be together.
And that's just the way it will be!"

A man walked in behind us.
His eyes were filled with grief.
He slowly took the last white rose
and pressed it to his cheek.

I didn't understand it then.
But now I realize.
That our "forevers" don't always last.
Only God gives eternal life.

Mom and Gram are
Here no more.

I'll miss them in this life.
But this one thing I am assured.
Someday, we will be
Together again.

*"...we have a building from God, an eternal
house in heaven, not built by human hands."
(II Corinthians 5:1-NIV)*

PART TWO

Challenging

The Path

Lord set me on that path
You have destined for me.
I promise to be faithful
And walk it diligently.

Let my steps be humble.
And dear God if I stumble.
Lift me to that higher ground.
Where Your grace and mercy abound.

 I will walk in Your statutes
All the days of my life.
I will not take my eyes off the prize.
I will not look left nor right.

But I will look to the hills
Where all my help comes from.
As I boldly tread that path
I've never walked before.

"I run in the path of Your commands,
for You have set my heart free."
(Psalm 119:32-NIV)

The Moment

Once it has happened
It can't be recaptured.

It can pass by unaware
Not to be found again.

One moment stands alone
As an entity by itself.

That cannot be stored
Like an item on a shelf.

Each precious moment counts
Each fleeting second stands.

As a reminder of how quickly
Time can slip through our hands.

*"Teach us to number our days
and recognize how few they are;
help us to spend them as we should."
(Psalm 90:12-Living Bible)*

Don't Waste Your Life

Chasing … after someone else's dream.
Pursuing …the world's material things.
Evading … the realities of life.
Consuming … sinful and evil desires.
Reliving … the mistakes from your past.
Seeking … the pleasures that do not last.
Forgetting … that your life has a purpose.
Ceasing … to believe in your self-worth.

Chase after God, **Pursue** Him, and you will find Him.
He will not **Evade** you, His love will **Consume** you, and
not allow you to **Relive** past failures. **Seek** Him with all
your heart. God will not **Forget** His plans and the
promises He has for you. His faithfulness is great and
His mercies will never **Cease**!

*"Do not conform any longer to the pattern of the world, but
be transformed by the renewing of your mind."
(Romans 12:2-NIV)*

Hidden Treasures

I pursue my vision
To the verge of success.
Renew my commitment
As I strive to do my best.

I can taste the victory
I have overcome defeat.
As I dwell in an atmosphere
Of victorious glee!

Then slowly but surely
The passion ebbs away.
Receding back into a sea
Of doing nothing days.

I stop pressing for the prize
As I set my gift aside.
Allowing it to lay dormant there,
On a shelf inside my mind.

Then I store it on the shelf
For no particular reason.
Where it remains unfruitful
For yet another season.

"If you wait for perfect conditions…
You will never get anything done."
(Ecclesiastes 11:4-Living Bible)

I Thought I Was Free

I dwelt outside the will of God.
I lived for pleasure alone.
No cares about tomorrow.
My life was on the run.

Everything was wonderful.
I thought I had it made.
I didn't even notice when
The lights began to fade.

Then one day unexpectedly
I didn't see it coming.
My life came tumbling down.
It only took a moment!

A foundation built on sand
Began to sink into the ground.
Of all the pleasures I had enjoyed
Only a remnant could be found.

I had to learn the hard way.
Material things don't last forever.
God's eternal love cannot be replaced
With earthly possessions that are temporary.

*"The world and its desires pass away, but the man
who does the will of God lives forever."
(1 John 2:17-NIV)*

Loose Ends

Loose ends have a way of unraveling our lives.
They come back to haunt us every time.
We meant to tuck them safely away.
To deal with them on another day.

From our unresolved relationships.
From apologies owed to delinquent debts.
From bitterness and unforgiveness.
From taking time to mend broken fences.

What started out as a very small matter.
Has now begun to multiply and scatter.
Wreaks havoc in our homes and lives.
Brings confusion to overwhelm our minds.

Loose ends don't go away by themselves.
They have a way of hanging around.
So tie up those knots you left open.
Don't put it off…deal with them now!

*"For God is closely watching you, and He
weighs carefully everything you do."
(Proverbs 5:21-Living Bible)*

Woulda, Coulda, Shoulda

Looking back on a situation.
Giving it much consideration.
I pondered over in my head
What I woulda, coulda, shoulda said.

At the time right words escaped me.
Choked up somewhere in my throat.
Instead this meaningless chatter
Began tumbling from my mouth.

Had I known this woulda happened
Then I coulda been prepared.
And not got caught off my guard.
Then I woulda known
What I shoulda said.

But when the conversation ended.
And as I quickly walked away.
I thought of at least a million things
I woulda, coulda, shoulda said!

"A word aptly spoken is like apples
of gold in settings of silver."
(Proverbs 25:11-NIV)

Be Yourself

Who are you trying to be today?
What role in life are you trying to play?
God created you to be unique.
An earthly display of His glory.

A counterfeiter is arrested.
A perpetrator is detested.
A pretender is most insincere.
An imitator is so un-for-real.

When its others you seek to please.
Heaven's reward you don't receive.
All of your works will be in vain
Praises of people are all you gain.

What you refuse to deal with.
Will always hold you back.
Pray for God to reveal it.
Let your denial be unmasked.

Search with eyes wide open.
The hidden issues of your heart.
Then you can stop living the life
Of someone you are not.

It's all about Him.
It's never about us.
It's who you know that He is.
And who He says that you are.

*"Casting down imaginations, and every high thing
that exalteth itself against the knowledge of God..."
(II Corinthians 10:5-KJV)*

Transparency

You know my comings and goings.
You see my thoughts from afar.
All my reaping…all my sowing.
The hidden issues in my heart.

Your gaze casts upon me.
A shining light into my soul.
It pierces the secret places.
Reveals the stories left untold.

It searches every motive.
It defines every intent.
Whether it is good or bad.
Self-serving or heaven sent.

"A man's conscience is the Lord's searchlight
exposing his hidden motives."
(Proverbs 20:27-KJV)

The Matters of the Heart

The matters of the heart.
We place them in Your hands.
But we get in a hurry
To take them back again.

The consequence we suffer.
A greater price to pay.
Because we should have waited
And not gotten in Your way.

Help us keep our eyes on You.
So our hearts won't lead us astray.
To know You are working things out
 In Your good and perfect way.

For Your timing is complete.
And Your victory is sweet.
There does exist no greater plan.
Than to place our cares into Your hands.

"But they that wait upon the Lord
shall renew their strength;
they shall mount up with wings like eagles;
they shall run, and not be weary, and
they shall walk, and not faint."
(Isaiah 40:31-KJV)

Mountains

God uses our mountains to exalt us
Far above our trials and troubles.
As His glory is revealed.
We behold His infinite power.

We are not to climb the mountain
Just to say we've reached the top.
And stake a flag there at its peak
Then declare a victorious shout!

God wants us to destroy it.
Remove it from our path.
To defeat and overcome it.
Never to face that mountain again!

*"... if you have faith as small as a mustard seed,
you can say to this mountain, 'Move from here to
there' and it will move. Nothing will be impossible
for you."*
(Matthew 17:20-NIV)

Yesterday

I was dwelling on my past.
Reviving some old hurts.
Jesus took me by the hand
And led me out of yesterday.

I had only meant to visit.
I did not intend to stay.
But some old familiar faces
Came by to help make my day.

Failure met me at the door.
Invited me in to have a seat.
Depression was there waiting,
And then began to remind me.

Of all the things I had lost.
Of all the things I cannot change.
The twins dropped by to see me.
Their names were guilt and shame.

God saw me getting weary.
So He took me by my hand.
And led me out of yesterday.
Back to my present land.

He reminded me of the promises
He has for me in store.
That my past had been forgiven.
That I had to let it go.

To dwell in the here and now.
To learn from days gone by.
To look forward to my future
And His destiny for my life.

"I, even I, am he who blots out your transgressions,
for my own sake, and remembers your sins
no more."
(Isaiah 43:25-NIV)

PART THREE

Encouraging

I Am an Original

I am an original.
I am unique.
God saw not another
When He created me.

He already knew
What my life would be about.
He had no questions.
He had no doubts.

I am not an imitation.
I cannot be replaced.
I am rare, I am special.
Fearfully...wonderfully made.

There was a purpose for my life
Before the portals of time.
And no one else can fulfill
What God has destined to be mine.

*"I praise You for I am fearfully
and wonderfully made...all the days
You ordained for me are written
in Your book."
(Psalm 139:14,16-NIV)*

Diamonds in the Rough

Far below the depths of earth
A precious stone lay covered.
Hidden beneath a layer of dirt
Waiting to be discovered.

Unaware that it was special.
Unique…one of a kind.
That it possessed great value.
God created it to shine.

So long it had existed
Of seeming little worth.
Denied of its potential.
The destiny it deserved.

It had to be dislodged
From its familiar place.
Washed and cleansed of dross
That bore a heavy weight.

Now the stone is beautiful
Radiant beyond compare.
Had it not been found
It would still be lying there.

We are these precious stones.
God is our master craftsman.
With jagged edges hewn
He refined us for His glory.

We were purchased with His blood
Worth more than silver or gold.
Designed to reflect His splendor.
We are God's diamonds in the rough.

"...you also, like living stones, are being
built into a spiritual house..."
(I Peter 2:5-NIV)

God Makes Everything Beautiful

God speaks into existence
His purpose in an instant.
He sets a thing in place
By His word…by His spirit.

He already knows
What you can't see ahead.
He already knows
The end of what begins.

When you do not see
Your desires come to pass.
It does not mean
That God does not care.

Do not be discouraged
His help is on its way.
God will bear you up
Your faith is not in vain.

God makes everything
Beautiful in His time.
In His own season
He reveals His glory divine.

For His own reason
He orders the steps in our lives.
As He makes everything
Beautiful in His time.

"He has made everything beautiful in its time.
He has also set eternity in the hearts of men; yet
they cannot fathom what God has done from
beginning to end."
(Ecclesiastes 3:11-NIV)

You Never Gave Up On Me

Sin had me bound
Under its heavy weight.
I had sank into a lowly state.
Your love broke the bonds
Of my captive gate.
You never gave up on me.

I wanted to give up.
Didn't count myself as worthy
Of Your forgiveness and love.
Felt someone else was more deserving.
When I thought that You were
Too far beyond my feeble reach.
You never gave up on me.

Your grace caused my heart to soar high.
Far above the limitations
I had placed upon my life.
You poured love into this empty vessel
And caused it to flow abundantly.
I am forever grateful that
You never gave up on me.

"...being confident of this, that He who began
a good work in you will carry it on to completion
until the day of Christ Jesus."
(Phillipians 1:6-NIV)

You Must Really Love Me

As unbelievable as it might seem.
Above my highest imagination.
Beyond my wildest dreams!
That You would take someone like me.
With all of my insecurities.
And love me unconditionally…
You must really love me!

It's hard for me to understand.
How I fit into your perfect plan.
I have failed You time and time again.
Stumbling blindly down life's paths!

Instead of reaching for Your hand.
I foolishly put my trust in man.
I didn't even give You a chance…
You must really love me!

To accept me as I am
Without any questions asked.
To give Your life for me.
Forgive me of my past.
Nothing can compare
To the grace that You have shown.
Your tender acts of mercy.
The compassion You bestow.
You must really love me!

"May the God of hope fill you with all joy
and peace as you trust in Him…"
(Romans 15:13-NIV)

Miracles

Have you ever felt like giving up?
Said that you are tired of trying
Felt like you have had enough?
Remember this before you do.
There is still a miracle
That could happen for you!

Feel your burden is too heavy to bear?
Thought that no one understands.
Sensed that no one really cares?
Many a person who has given up
Will miss their chance to find out...
What could have happened
What could have been
If only they had not given in.

You never know unless you try.
There might be risks you have to take.
But at least you gave it all you had.
Your miracle could happen any day!

*"No eye has seen, no ear has heard, no mind has conceived
what God has prepared for those who love him..."
(1 Corinthians 2:9-NIV)*

Keep On Walking

When the pain is
Just too much to bear.
And many have left
Who said they'd be there.
And others don't seem
To share your cares,
Don't give up…keep on walking.

Though times are hard
And the chips are down.
The road is narrow
You stumble and fall.
Get up! Shake it off!
God can turn it around,
Don't stop…keep on walking.

Trials will come and go
Life is not always fair.
Don't try to figure it out
When you can't understand.
Put your faith in motion
Don't look back at your trouble.
Place one foot in front of the other,
And keep on walking!

"Trust in the Lord with all thine heart; and lean
not unto thine own understanding…"
(Proverbs 3:5-NIV)

A Kind Word Spoken

A kind word spoken
In a time of need.
Can heal a broken heart.
Speak life to a dying dream.

Can flood a ray of sunshine
Into a cloudy day.
Can cause a smile to spread
Across a weary face.

Can turn a drop of tears
Into a shout of joy.
Can give someone back their hope.
That they believed was gone.

"..he who refreshes others will
himself be refreshed."
(Proverbs 11:25-NIV)

I Believe in Miracles

A wheel chair… folded away in the corner.
Its days of usefulness are now over.

A pair of crutches… laid gathering dust.
No longer needed to provide support.

A report from the doctor… only months to live.
Is reversed and life expectancy is fulfilled.

A young wife's prayer… to heal her barren womb.
Is answered with the news of a baby coming soon.

A broken marriage… tears a family apart.
Is now restored by the mending of shattered hearts.

A job was lost…the mortgage was overdue.
A new job came along…with a financial blessing too.

This is not just a dream.
This is not my imagination.
With my own eyes I have seen.
The working of God's intervention.

Just when it had seemed
That there was no way out.
God stepped in with a miracle
And turned these situations around.

"Now unto Him that is able to do exceedingly,
abundantly, above all that we ask or think
according to the power that worketh in us."
(Ephesians 3:20-KJV)

The Giver of Care

The assurance from a smile
That says you understand.
The comfort that you give
With the touch of your hand.

On shoulders strong
You bear the weight
That they can't carry
When their strength is weak.

Throughout the day you weigh every sigh.
Your ears are attuned to their groans in the night.
You grow accustomed to little if any sleep.
While one eye shuts the other eye peeps.

Their well being and safety is your great concern.
Your ever watchful eyes carefully discern.
With doctors and nurses you have to contend.
With answers to questions you don't understand.

Trying to be strong for the both of you.
While trusting in God to guide you through.
With loving dedication you go about your day.
You wouldn't have it any other way.

Be strong, be encouraged
God only allows what you can bear.
He will never forsake you
His grace is sufficient for you...
The Giver of Care.

"Wait on the Lord: be of good courage, and He
shall strengthen thine heart:..."
(Psalm 27:14-KJV)

We Stand As One

We stand together as one
Anchored and secured.
Our faith is strong.
It is firm, unshakable.

We stand together as one
Planted like a tree.
Though fierce winds blow.
We are not moved by what we see.

He will not leave us
To face this battle alone.
We will stand on God's promises
We will stand together as one.

*"For where two or three come together
in My name, there am I with them."
(Matthew 18:20-NIV)*

CONCLUSION

As long as we live...there will be trials. From every trial there is a lesson that is learned...there is faith that is anchored...there is power that is unleashed... there is authority that is established. God allows us to see all of these qualities working in us, and we then use them as spiritual weapons for our battle.

Sometimes the worst things that happen to us can help to bring out the best things that are in us.

LaVergne, TN USA
04 December 2009

166034LV00003B/4/P

9 781600 473753